Sit

by Cecilia Winters
illustrated by Kate Flanagan

Core Decodable 11

McGraw Hill Education

Bothell, WA • Chicago, IL • Columbus, OH • New York, NY

MHEonline.com

Send all inquiries to:
McGraw-Hill Education
8787 Orion Place
Columbus, OH 43240

ISBN: 978-0-02-145565-2
MHID: 0-02-145565-1

Printed in Canada.

9 10 11 12 KOD 24

Sid, Sis, and Tim sit.

Did Matt sit? See Matt stand.

Sid and Sis sit.

Did Tim sit? See Tim stand.

Did Sid sit? Did Sis sit?

Sid did it! Sid sits.